Growing Readers

Purchased with Smart Start Funds

Walk Around

A Town

Peter and Connie Roop

Heinemann Library
Des Plaines, Illinois

Designed by Lindaanne Donohoe
Printed in Hong Kong

03 02 01 00 99 99
10 9 8 7 6 5 4 3 2 1

Library of Congress Cataloging-in-Publication Data

Roop, Peter.
    A town / Peter and Connie Roop.
        p. cm. – (Walk around)
    Includes bibliographical references and index.
    Summary: Describes the transportation, schools, housing, shopping,
working, recreations, and other aspects of life in a typical American
town, using Elkton, Maryland, as an example.
    ISBN 1-57572-128-7
    1. Cities and towns—United States—Juvenile literature. 2. City
and town life—Maryland—Elkton—Juvenile literature. [1. Cities
and towns. 2. City and town life. 3. Elkton (Md.)] I. Roop.
Connie. II. Title. III. Series: Roop, Peter. Walk around.
HT123.R64733 1998
307.76'0973—dc21   98-14918
                                                              CIP
                                                               AC

Acknowledgments
All photographs by Phil Martin except those listed below.

Cover photograph: Phil Martin

The author and publishers are grateful to the following for permission to reproduce
copyright photographs:
Tony Stone Images/David Barnes, p. 4 (Leadville); Ryan-Beyer, p. 5 (Pella); ©Tony Stone Images,
Inc./Don Valentine, p. 5 (Rockport); Adelma Gregory, pp. 28–29.

Every effort has been made to contact copyright holders of any material reproduced
in this book. Any omissions will be rectified in subsequent printings if notice is given
to the publisher.

Some words are shown in bold, **like this.** You can find out what they mean by looking
in the glossary.

For Tristan, who got us walking around.

Contents

What Is a Town?

Leadville, Colorado

A town is a **community** that is not part of a large city's **metropolitan area.** Some towns only have a few hundred people. Other towns have thousands of **citizens.** No matter what the size, all towns are different. Different people, buildings, and activities help make each town special.

Rockport, Massachusetts

Pella, Iowa

Elkton, Maryland

Mapping the Town

Most Towns have a **business district.** This is usually on a **main street.** Business districts have stores, offices, and restaurants.

Outside the business district are areas where people live. On the roads leading into town are large supermarkets and **department stores.** This map shows Elkton, Maryland, the town you are walking around in this book. About ten thousand people live in Elkton.

Elkton

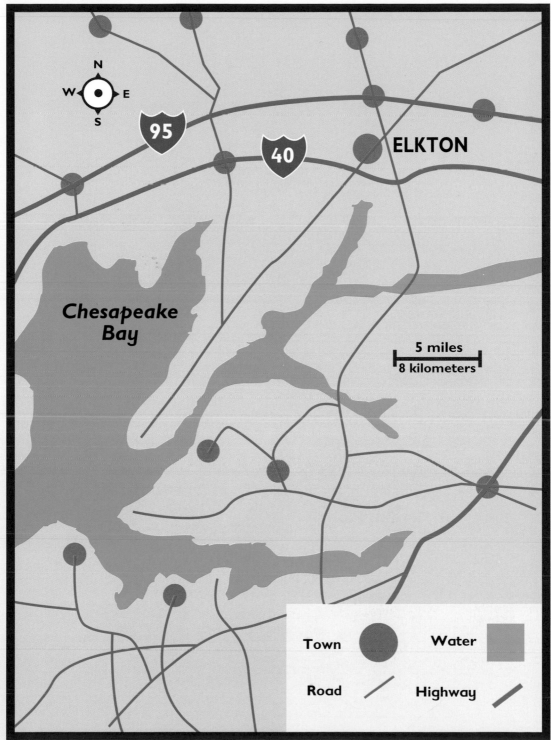

Chesapeake Bay

5 miles
8 kilometers

ELKTON

95

40

Town

Water

Road

Highway

Homes

Most homes in a town are houses. These houses are within walking distance of the **business district.**

People also live in rows of homes or **town houses.** Some people live in apartments above stores in the business district.

Getting Around

Places in a town are usually close together. People drive, walk, or ride bikes to get where they want. Most towns don't have **public transportation** like cities do.

People park their cars along the street and walk to the stores in the **business district.**

Schools

Because towns don't have many people, there is usually only one elementary school, one middle school, and one high school. Students walk, ride bikes, or ride in cars and buses to get to school.

Many schools are surrounded by houses.
Most children know many of the other kids in
their school.

The Police

Towns usually have one police station, but many officers work there.

Police officers help in many ways. They protect the town, teach **citizens** about safety, and use computers to send and get important information.

Working

Most people work in or near the town. Some people help build new roads and buildings. Others are farmers. Some people help run the town.

Citizens also work in factories like this one outside of town. Most towns have many small stores, shops, and restaurants. These businesses are usually owned and run by people who live in the **community.**

Shopping

In the **business district,** there are many small stores. People who work in the business district can shop here during the day. These stores usually close when the workers go home.

Some towns also have a large **strip mall** on a highway going out of town. These malls may have a large supermarket or **department store** and other smaller stores. The stores usually stay open late.

The Library

A town has one library. People borrow books, do research, and can find information about the **community** there.

Besides books, libraries have computers
and CD-ROMs for people to use and learn
from. Librarians often know what some
people enjoy reading. They will search for
those materials and let a person know if
they find something special.

Banks and Money

Towns usually have two or three banks. These banks help **community** businesses with their money. Banks **lend** money to businesses so they can build bigger buildings or buy more products to sell.

Many banks have drive-up windows so people can do their banking while waiting in their cars. There are also cash machines at supermarkets where people can get money.

The Post Office

There is one post office in town where people mail letters and packages and buy stamps. People can also use the drive-up mailbox to mail letters.

Letter carriers deliver mail to offices, apartment buildings, businesses, and homes. Letter carriers drive or walk their routes.

Playing

Most towns have several parks. The parks are used for different activities. People may use one park for picnics. Other parks might have soccer fields or basketball courts.

Most towns have sports leagues. Children of all ages can play with and against their friends. Some towns have a movie theater. A town museum may teach **citizens** about the history of their town.

Helping Out

Citizens of a town know not only their neighbors, but many other people in the town as well. People care deeply about their friends and the **community**.

People in a town help each other. Many students help build new homes for families in need. Others plant trees and help keep the town clean. Projects like these help build the community and make people feel proud of where they live.

Glossary

business district area in the middle of a town with many businesses

citizens people who live in a city or town

community area where people live, work, and shop

department stores large stores that sell many different things

lend to let someone use something and then return it later

main street most important street in town

metropolitan area area that includes a large city and its suburbs

public transportation ways of travel that are organized and that everyone can use

strip mall one long building divided into many different stores

town houses many homes connected together

More Books to Read

Around Town. New York: DK Publishing, 1995.

Baylor, Byrd. *The Best Town in the World*. New York: Simon & Schuster Children's, 1983.

Coster, Patience. *Towns and Cities*. Danbury, Conn: Children's Press, 1998.

Fitzpatrick, Shanon. *Communities*. Cypress, Cal: Creative Teaching Press, 1995.

Gutman, Bill. *In Your Neighborhood*. New York: Henry Holt & Company, 1996.

Provensen, Alice and Martin. *Town and Country*. Orlando, Fla: Browndeer Press (Harcourt Brace), 1994.

Index